SPECIFICATIONS AND TOLERANCES

for Reference Standards and Field Standard Weights and Measures

NIST

United States
Department of
Commerce

Technology
Services

National Institute
of Standards and
Technology

8. Specifications and Tolerances
for Field Standard Weight Carts

NIST
Handbook 105-8

2003

SPECIFICATIONS AND TOLERANCES

for Reference Standards and Field Standard Weights and Measures

8. Specifications and Tolerances for Field Standard Weight Carts

NIST Weight Cart Working Group

Editor:
Val Miller

Henry V. Oppermann, Chief
National Institute of Standards and Technology
Weights and Measures Division
Gaithersburg, MD 20899

October 2003

U.S. DEPARTMENT OF COMMERCE
Donald L. Evans, Secretary
TECHNOLOGY ADMINISTRATION
Phillip J. Bond, Under Secretary of Commerce for Technology
NATIONAL INSTITUTE OF STANDARDS AND TECHNOLOGY
Arden L. Bement, Jr., Director

NIST Handbook **105-8**

2003

Preface

Acknowledgement:
The editor wishes to thank Ronald Balaze, Michigan Department of Agriculture and Georgia Harris, NIST Weights and Measures Division for their development of the first draft of this handbook in 1998. Thanks must be given the members of the NIST Weight Cart Working Group for their work in developing a standard for field standard weight carts.

The working group included:
Val Miller, NIST Office of Weights and Measures (Chair)
Georgia Harris, NIST Office of Weights and Measures
Bruce Adams, Minnesota Department of Commerce
David Ehrnschwender, Fairbanks Scales, Inc.
Emil Hazarian, Los Angeles County Agricultural Commissioner Weights and Measures Department
John Dewald, Tiffin Loader Crane
John Holt, Kanawha Scales and Systems, Inc.
L.F. Eason, North Carolina Department of Agriculture and Consumer Services
Richard Suiter, NIST Office of Weights and Measures
Ronald Balaze, Michigan Department of Agriculture
Sid Colbrook, Illinois Department of Agriculture Bureau of Weights and Measures
Tom Schafer, Idaho Department of Agriculture Bureau of Weights and Measures

Thanks must also be expressed to those members of the State Weights and Measures community who read the draft standard and provided constructive feedback to further improve the document. Without the input of potential users of field standard weight carts, this standard could not provide the balance between usability in the field and metrological integrity that has been achieved.

The use of Field Standard Weight Carts in testing large capacity scales is a complex and sometimes emotional issue. Weight cart use permits one or two individuals to test a large capacity scale in a fraction of the time required by previous methods of testing. They allow the scale inspector or technician to load the weights required for the test into the weight cart and then move it to various positions on the scale deck, with a single handling of the weights. This results in tremendous time savings, which converts to similar savings in manpower costs and downtime for the scale operator.

However, there are many sources of variability in weight carts used for scale calibrations. Variability sources include but are not limited to such items as consumable liquids used as fuel for liquid fueled engines, engine lubricating oil, hydraulic fluid, and also contamination by dirt, mud and/or water. There are also forces that are potentially destructive to the scale under test generated by the concentration of large amounts of weight on the small contact patch of rubber-tired wheels. The members of the working group addressed each of these issues.

Contents

Specifications and Tolerances
for Reference Standards and Field Standard
Weights and Measures

8. Specifications and Tolerances for Field Standard Weight Carts

These specifications and tolerances are recommended as minimum requirements for standards used by State and local weights and measures officials and others in the verification of large capacity scales used in quantity determination of commodities by means of weighing.

Key words: weight cart; retroactivity; field standard weight cart; specification; standard; scale; tolerance; scale specifications and tolerances; weights and measures.

Introduction
A field standard weight cart (after this, simply called "weight cart") is intended for use in conjunction with Class F weights for testing commercial weighing devices for compliance with the requirements of NIST Handbook 44. The combination of Class F weights and weight cart may be used to test class III and III L scales with a division size ('d') equal to or greater than 5 lb, class IIII scales, and scales not marked with a class designation with a 'd' equal to or greater than 5 lb.

Compliance with this standard does not guarantee suitability of a weight cart to test a specific weighing device at all specified test loads. Each test load to be used must be evaluated for compliance with the requirements of NIST Handbook 44, Appendix A, "Fundamental Considerations," Section 3, "Testing Apparatus." This section of Handbook 44 establishes the minimum requirements for the standards used in legal metrology, including a statement that the maximum error of an uncorrected standard should not exceed one-third of the smallest tolerance for the device tested.[1]

1 Scope
1.1 'Field Standard' Classification
These specifications are limited to motorized weight carts used in conjunction with NIST Handbook 105-1, Class F field standard weights. Weight carts are NOT considered NIST Class F field standards. This handbook does not apply to railroad test cars or non-motorized weight baskets.

1.2 Retroactivity
These specifications apply to new weight carts manufactured after the effective date of this publication (September 2003).

A weight cart in service before the publication of this standard that maintains tolerance between verification tests shall continue to be acceptable, though some modifications may be required for

---

[1] Equation to be used: $T_{cart} + T_{weights} < \dfrac{T_{scale}}{3}$

continued acceptability under this standard. All weight carts in service must comply with those specifications that have an asterisk (*) following the title. These include requirements addressing tires, batteries, tolerances and fuel tanks. Existing components that comply with the requirements are acceptable for continued use. Weight carts in service at the time of this publication that do not conform to required sections, must be brought into compliance by December 31, 2005.

Weights and measures jurisdictions may require that a weight cart comply with non-retroactive specifications, if additional modifications are required to maintain a weight cart within tolerance. Weight carts that do not maintain the specified tolerance shall be removed from service until modifications are performed that enable the weight cart to maintain tolerance.

1.3 Safety Considerations
The use of weight carts may involve hazardous materials, conditions, operations and equipment. This document does not purport to address the safety problems associated with weight cart use.

Known hazards may include, but are not limited to:
- The handling of petroleum products,
- The handling and connection or disconnection of energized electrical cables,
- The use, maintenance and disposal of various types of batteries,
- Handling of large weights, and
- Possible exposure to carbon monoxide fumes from gasoline engine exhaust.

It is the responsibility of the user to establish appropriate safety and health practices and to determine the applicability of regulatory limitations prior to use.

1.4 Units
The majority of scales tested with weight carts indicate mass values in U.S. Customary units. Petroleum products used in weight carts have a 60 °F (15.56 °C) reference temperature. Therefore, this publication primarily uses U.S. Customary units due to the needs of industry and regulators. Metric equivalents are provided when the likelihood exists that they may be used. Metric equivalent values provided may not be exact conversions but are provided as convenient alternative values that will not have an adverse impact on the quality of the scale calibrations.

2 Reference Documents
2.1 NIST[2]
NIST Handbook 44, Specifications, Tolerances, and Other Technical Requirements for Weighing and Measuring Devices, (current edition)

NIST Handbook 105-1, Specifications and Tolerances for Field Standard Weights (NIST Class F)

NIST Handbook 112, Examination Procedure Outlines for Weighing and Measuring Devices

---

[2] NIST, National Institute of Standards and Technology

2.2 NCWM[3]

NCWM Publication 3, NCWM Policy and Guidelines, Section 3.2.15, 1991.

NCWM Publication 14, National Type Evaluation Program, (NTEP) Administrative Procedures, Technical Policy, Checklists, and Test Procedures, see current edition, published annually.

3 Terminology

Class F Field Standard Weight. A weight meeting NIST Handbook 105-1 design, construction and tolerance criteria for field standards.

Field Standard. The term "field standard" means the physical standards that meet specifications and tolerances in NIST 105-series handbooks (where available) having calibrated measurement results traceable to primary or secondary standards through comparisons using accepted laboratory procedures.

Tolerance. Maximum permissible error. A value fixing the limit of allowable error or departure from the true performance or value.

T_{cart}. Tolerance of empty weight cart.

$T_{weights}$. Tolerance for NIST Class F field standard weights used to supplement the weight cart to achieve a given test load in scale testing, from NIST HB 105-1.

T_{scale}. Tolerance of the scale at the test load, from HB 44.

Weight cart. A field standard test weight meeting the requirements of NIST Handbook 105-8 used both as a field standard weight and as the means of moving NIST Class F field standard weights before, during and after, large capacity scale tests.

4 General Specifications
4.1 Weight
4.1.1 Nominal Empty Weight

Weight carts shall be constructed in one of the following 500 lb (226.80 kg) increments: 2000 lb (907.18 kg), 2500 lb (1133.98 kg), 3000 lb (1360.78 kg), 3500 lb (1587.57 kg), 4000 lb (1814.37 kg), 4500 lb (2041.17 kg), 5000 lb (2267.96 kg), 5500 lb (2494.76 kg) or 6000 lb (2721.55 kg). Suitability for the intended application should be considered before selecting a nominal value.

The weight cart, with the adjustment cavity empty and all fluid levels adjusted to the reference levels, shall weigh a minimum of 50 lb and a maximum of 100 lb less than the nominal empty weight.

---

[3] NCWM, National Conference on Weights and Measures

The manufacturer will supply each new weight cart with sufficient adjustment material to bring the weight cart to its nominal mass.

4.1.2 Weight and Size Limitations

Local weights and measures jurisdictions may have use, size or weight restrictions on weight carts. Approval of use, size and weight must be obtained from the weights and measures jurisdiction(s) in which weight cart use is planned. Coordination between the purchaser and the supporting calibration laboratory is essential, before purchase, to ensure that the laboratory can provide a proper calibration.

4.2 Materials

A weight cart body and frame shall be constructed of steel. Other durable and stable materials may be developed, but approval for use of such materials must be obtained from the NIST Weights and Measures Division or local Weights and Measures agency prior to use of alternative construction materials.

Rubber hoses may be utilized for fluid transfer where flexible connections are needed, but should be kept to a minimum. Metallic tubing is to be used where possible to minimize use of rubber hoses.

4.3 Workmanship, Finish, and Appearance

All edges and corners shall be smooth, with no sharp edges, to prevent injury during routine use and maintenance. All surfaces shall be free from slag, scale and weld splatter, grit, dirt, or any foreign matter before shipment from the factory or before submission for calibration.

Unless constructed of corrosion resistant materials, all exposed surfaces shall have a protective surface coating. The coating must be a high quality material having the following properties: corrosion inhibiting, chip and abrasion resistant, smooth surface and non-hygroscopic. Flat aluminum paint or flat lacquer finishes are preferred.

4.4 Design

Representative designs are shown in Figures 1 and 2; variations in design are permitted. Prior to production, manufacturers should seek design approval from NIST Weights and Measures Division. 'Design approval' applies only to the size and suitability of the cart as a field standard in the calibration of large capacity scales, and will not in any way imply design approval for structural strength and integrity.

4.5 Identification Plate
4.5.1 Placement

Each weight cart shall have an identification plate permanently mounted in a conspicuous and easily accessible place near the operator controls.

4.5.2   Content

The identification plate shall contain the following items in clear permanent text in a font size no smaller than 0.1 in by 0.1 in (2.5 mm by 2.5 mm).

- Nominal empty weight of the cart;
- Maximum gross weight;
- Name and address of the manufacturer;
- Manufacturer's model number;
- Manufacturer's unique serial or identification number;
- Date of manufacture;
- Statement of compliance with NIST HB 105-8 including the revision in effect at time of manufacture; and
- Additional information that the manufacturer may deem necessary.

4.6   Power

Weight carts may be powered by an electric motor (battery or generator driven), or liquid fueled engine. Power may be transmitted to the wheels by either fluid or mechanical coupling methods.

4.7   Fuel Tank *
4.7.1   Capacity, Shape and Mounting

Liquid fueled weight carts shall have a maximum total fuel capacity of 1-gallon (231 in^3 or 3785 cm^3) when filled to the fuel tank reference level. Of this volume, a minimum of 0.72 gallons (167 in^3 or 2740 cm^3) shall cause an indication in the sight gauge. The fuel tank shall have the general shape of an upright cylinder and shall comply with all applicable state and federal regulations. The fuel tank shall be permanently attached to the weight cart structure so that the gauge assembly is positioned vertically. The fuel tank shall be mounted on the weight cart structure away from heated components such as the engine exhaust so that refueling does not constitute an unnecessary safety hazard. The top of the fuel tank, when mounted to the weight cart, shall not extend above the plane described by the top edge of the weight restraint system. A representative fuel tank design is shown in Attachment 1; approved variations of this design are permitted. Prior to production, manufacturers should obtain the approval of the NIST Weights and Measures Division for new fuel tank designs. New designs should be submitted to the Weights and Measures Division, National Institute of Standards and Technology, Gaithersburg, MD 20899.

The fuel tank shall be identified with a unique serial number permanently etched or stamped into the tank near the fill cap

4.7.2   Cross Sectional Area of Tank

The combined cross sectional area of the fuel tank and sight gauge must be no greater than 12.8 in^2 (82.33 cm^2) at all liquid levels within the graduated range.

4.7.3   Fuel Tank Material

The fuel tank shall be constructed of low carbon or corrosion resistant steel. Non-integral hardware may be constructed of other materials provided the material is durable and suitable for its intended purpose.

4.7.4　Fuel Tank Color and Finish

The fuel tank shall be light in color to minimize heating of the fuel by radiant heat sources. Any plating or paint materials shall not be degraded by contact with the fuel. A natural stainless steel color is acceptable.

4.7.5　Fuel Tank Drain

If the fuel tank is equipped with a fuel tank drain apparatus, the assembly must extend past the edge of any nearby weight cart structure.

4.7.6　Gauge Assembly
4.7.6.1　Gauge Tube
4.7.6.1.1　Material

Weight cart fuel tanks shall be equipped with a (liquid-level) gauge tube mounted on the tank body in plain view of the weight cart operator. The gauge tube shall be made of a transparent material such as borosilicate glass, be clear and free of any markings, irregularities or defects which will distort the appearance of the liquid surface. Clarity of the gauge tube material shall not be degraded by contact with the fuel. The gauge tube may be coated to prevent fuel spillage in case of tube breakage, provided the coating material is clear and free of markings, irregularities or defects that will distort the appearance of the liquid surface and is not degraded by contact with the fuel.

4.7.6.1.2　Mounting

The gauge tube shall be mounted in fittings which penetrate the tank body near the base and as near the top as possible (to allow passage of vapors from the tube for vapor recovery purposes). Fittings shall be designed so that all fuel and vapor are returned to the fuel tank and no spillage can occur. The fitting at the top of the tube may have a removable plug so the tube can be cleaned. However, this plug opening must be sealed during weight cart operation. The plug shall not interfere with proper vapor equalization (i.e., it shall not allow pressure build up to affect the liquid level in the gauge). Removal and replacement of the tube shall be possible and the metal to glass seal shall be made leak proof by the use of compressible gaskets or "O" rings.

4.7.6.2　Shield

On fuel tanks where protection of the tube is provided by a shield or cover, the design of the cover shall allow replacement of the gauge tube with ease and shall facilitate gauge reading by the weight cart operator.

4.7.6.3　Scale Plate and Graduations
4.7.6.3.1　Material

The scale plate shall be rigid and resistant to corrosion and discoloration (anodized aluminum or stainless steel).

4.7.6.3.2　Location

The scale plate shall be mounted on a secant to the front of, or slightly in front of the gauge tube. In no case shall the scale plate be more than 0.25 in (6 mm) from the tube.

4.7.6.3.3 Mounting

There shall be a sufficient number of scale brackets (minimum of two) to hold the scale plate rigidly in place. The scale plate shall be securely attached to the brackets and be provided with a means for sealing.

4.7.6.3.4 Scale Units

The basic units on fuel tank scale plates shall be pounds of fuel, based on the average density of the fuel used at the API[4] reference temperature of 60 °F (15.56 °C). The reference density to be used[5]: Gasoline: 6.213 lb/gal (API 58.38), and diesel: 7.113 lb/gal (API 34.35). The scale plate shall be clearly marked as to the unit of measure with the header text "Add lb." to indicate the amount of weight required to return the weight cart to its nominal weight with the indicated fuel load. Graduated scale plates shall be made of a single piece of material and adjusted and sealed as a unit.

4.7.6.3.5 Graduation Spacing

The minimum distance between adjacent graduation lines shall be 0.0625 in (2 mm), and the lines shall be evenly spaced.

4.7.6.3.6 Span of Graduations

The sight gauge scale plate shall be graduated at a reference (zero) line with major graduations at 0.5 lb increments with sub-graduations at 0.25 lb increments below the reference line, over the length of the sight gauge. The reference line shall be approximately 1 inch from the top of the gauge tube. The distance between the markings shall be established based on the fuel tank cross-sectional area and the API value for the recommended fuel.

4.7.6.3.7 Scale Lines

The graduation lines, numbers, and other inscriptions on the scale plate shall be engraved, etched or silk screened, permanent, and of a contrasting color to that of the plate.

4.7.6.3.8 Line Spacing and Width

Major graduation lines, consistent with the measurement system used, shall be longer than sub-graduation lines and shall be appropriately numbered. The length of the major (numbered) graduation lines on the scale plate shall be no less than 0.25 in (6 mm), and the sub-graduation lines shall be no less than 0.125 in (3 mm) in length. All lines shall extend to the edge of the scale plate nearest the gauge tube. Graduation lines shall be of uniform width and not more than 0.025 inches (0.6 mm) or less than 0.015 inches (0.4 mm) wide.

4.7.6.3.9 Volume Reference Marking

The reference volume line on the scale plate shall extend across the entire width of the scale plate and shall be clearly identified. Each 0.5 lb graduation shall be appropriately labeled to indicate the mass of the fuel required to return the fuel level to the reference line.

---

[4] American Petroleum Institute
[5] Based on 2001-2002 fuel data obtained from Northrop Grumman Petroleum Technologies, Bartlesville, OK

4.7.6.3.10   Additional Markings
Scale plates shall be clearly marked with the fuel tank manufacturer's name, the fuel tank serial number, type of fuel and fuel density (lb/gal) for which it is intended. Letters and numbers shall be legible and of adequate size, not less than 0.1 inches (2.5 mm) in height.

4.7.7   Tolerances (Maximum Permissible Error)
The difference between the actual volume and any indicated volume at the prescribed reference temperature, 60 °F (15.56 °C), shall not be greater than ± 2 in^3 (32.8 cm^3) based on the assumed reference fuel density as stated in section 4.7.6.3.4.

4.7.8   Fuel Tank Initial and Periodic Verification
Weight cart fuel tank scale plate graduations must undergo initial verification for conformance to these specification and tolerances during the initial calibration of the weight cart, prior to placing the weight cart into service, and when damage is suspected. Routine calibration of the fuel tanks is not recommended. Initial fuel tank verification may be conducted by the fuel tank or weight cart manufacturer provided a certificate of conformance to the applicable sections of NIST HB 105-8 is provided with the fuel tank. The fuel tank certificate of conformance must indicate the fuel tank manufacturer's name and address, fuel tank serial number, the standard(s) used for calibration, the expanded uncertainty of the calibration process, a statement of measurement traceability, and identification of the individual performing the verification. The fuel tank conformance certificate shall become part of the weight cart maintenance log.

NOTE: The described certificate of conformance does not meet the requirements of ISO/IEC 17025 for an accredited calibration. An accredited calibration of the weight cart may require that an accredited laboratory perform the one-time fuel tank verification.

4.7.9   Fuel Tank Verification Method
Verification to determine whether a weight cart fuel tank meets applicable tolerances is performed by calibration using accepted volumetric calibration procedures. The uncertainty of the test method must be less than one-third of the tolerance.

4.7.10   Fuel Level Error Weights
The manufacturer of a liquid fueled weight cart shall supply sufficient 0.5 lb error weights (and a separate carrying case) to compensate for the fuel tank capacity visible on the sight gauge. A means shall be provided (e.g., a basket or hook arrangement) whereby the operator can easily and securely attach the 0.5 lb error weights to the weight cart structure to compensate for weight lost as liquid fuel is expended. The mounting arrangement shall securely restrain the Fuel Level Error Weights to prevent them from vibrating. The error weights shall be placed on the weight cart structure only when required to compensate for expended fuel. The Fuel Level Error Weights shall conform to tolerances and specifications contained in NIST Handbook 105-1, "Specifications and Tolerances for Field Standard Weights (NIST Class F)."

4.8 Hydraulic Fluid System
4.8.1 Hydraulic Fluid Reservoir Fluid Level Indicator
Weight carts equipped with a hydraulic reservoir must have a sight gauge, with a clearly marked reference level, for maintaining hydraulic fluid levels. The fluid level must be visible under all operating conditions. The hydraulic reservoir shall have sufficient expansion capacity so that no hydraulic fluid will be lost during normal use. The fluid level shall be adjusted to the reference level with the hydraulic fluid temperature at calibration laboratory conditions (18 °C to 27 °C).

4.8.2 Hydraulic Fluid Reservoir Fluid Fill and Drain Tamper Indicators
The fill and drain caps of the hydraulic reservoir shall be equipped so that a wire seal can be installed to indicate tampering with or adjustment of the hydraulic fluid level. Tampering or adjustment requires that the weight cart be submitted for recalibration prior to use as a field standard.

4.8.3 Hydraulic Fluid Reservoir Fluid Drain System
If equipped with a hydraulic fluid reservoir drain apparatus, the drain assembly must extend past the edge of any nearby weight cart structure.

4.8.4 Hydraulic Fluid Filtration System
The hydraulic fluid filter system shall be positioned, or a suitable means developed, so that removal does not cause oily contamination of any fixed cart surfaces.

4.9 Engine Lubricating Oil System (if equipped with an internal combustion engine)
4.9.1 Engine Lubricating Oil Reservoir Reference Level
The lubricating oil reservoir of the weight cart engine shall be maintained at the reference level established by the engine manufacturer using the recommended lubricating oil type. The lubricating oil level shall be adjusted, prior to calibration or use, to the reference level with the oil temperature between 18 °C and 27 °C (64 °F and 81 °F). The engine must not have been operated for a period of at least 4 hours immediately prior to adjustment of the engine oil level. Significant contamination by fuel or combustion deposits shall require that the lubricating oil be replaced and that the cart be recalibrated.

4.9.2 Engine Lubricating Oil Reservoir Drain System
If equipped with a lubricating oil reservoir drain apparatus, the drain assembly must extend past the edge of any nearby weight cart structure.

4.9.3 Engine Lubricating Oil Filter
The engine oil filter shall be positioned, or a suitable means developed, so that removal does not cause oil contamination of any fixed cart surfaces.

4.10 Engine Exhaust
The exhaust pipe(s) shall be positioned and/or shielded so that the operator does not come in contact with them during normal weight cart operation. Exhaust gasses shall exit the exhaust pipe(s) in a horizontal direction and shall be directed away from the operator control station.

4.11 Tires *
4.11.1 Size and Number
Tire size and quantity shall be chosen to prevent scale platform contact pressures that exceed design limitations. The total contact area of the tires to the supporting surface shall cause no point load concentrations in excess of 200 lb/in^2 (1.38 MPa) when loaded to the maximum gross capacity of the weight cart.

4.11.2 Tire Tread Pattern
Weight cart tire surfaces shall be smooth (without tread) and have no major cuts or deformations.

4.12 Wheel Bearings
Axle bearing/hub assemblies should not require routine lubrication. Where possible, the use of sealed prelubricated bearings is recommended. Bearing units requiring liquid lubricants are not permitted.

4.13 Minimum Wheelbase and Track Dimensions
The weight cart shall be designed so that the center of gravity in any loading configuration shall not cause the weight cart to become unstable on slopes normally encountered during scale testing.

4.14 Drainage
Weight carts shall be designed to prevent the pooling of water on weight cart surfaces. Horizontal surfaces of the cart must be constructed of a single layer of material to prevent weight instability caused by trapped water layers.

4.15 Weight Restraint
Weight carts shall be permanently equipped with a weight restraint system suitable for the weights being used to restrain all test weights being transported during scale testing.

4.16 Weight Cart Transport
It is strongly recommended that weight carts be transported in an enclosed truck body to prevent contamination of the weight cart. As a minimum, the weight cart shall be covered by a suitable waterproof covering during transport. The weight cart shall have provision to be securely fastened to the transporting vehicle while being transported.

4.17 Lifting Attach Points
4.17.1 Lifting Attach Points Purpose
The weight cart shall be equipped with a means of lifting the empty weight cart onto a transport vehicle and onto a scale or balance for calibration.

4.17.2 Weight Cart Balance
The empty weight cart shall balance in an approximately level position when lifted by the means specified by the manufacturer.

4.18 Adjustment Cavities

Weight carts shall be designed with one or more adjustment cavities. Multiple adjustment cavities are permitted when required for adjusting the balance of the weight cart when lifted in the manner specified by the manufacturer. Adjustment cavities must be designed to prevent water penetration/contamination.

4.18.1 Cavity Capacity

Weight cart adjustment cavities shall have a minimum total capacity of approximately 150 lb of adjustment material.

4.18.2 Adjustment Cavity Mounting

Adjustment cavities must be removable for performing weight adjustment activities. Adjustment cavities shall be securely attached to the main weight cart structure and configured so that a wire seal or other suitable tamper indicator can be installed to indicate tampering.

4.18.3 Adjustment Cavity Opening(s)

Adjustment cavity opening(s) shall be easily accessible, sufficiently large and positioned to facilitate the insertion and removal of adjustment materials. Adjustment cavity openings shall be watertight.

Each adjustment cavity opening shall have provision for sealing with a wire seal, or other suitable seal to indicate tampering.

4.18.4 Adjustment Material

Any metal in the form of shot or solid pieces may be used in adjustment cavities to adjust the weight of the cart. Lead or steel shot is preferred. Molten metals are not permitted.

4.19 Brakes
4.19.1 Service Brake

Weight carts shall be designed with a braking device or system that allows the operator to restrain the fully loaded cart when descending slopes, and to bring the weight cart to a smooth stop when desired. The service brake must maintain the weight cart in position until released by the operator.

4.19.2 Parking Brake

Weight carts shall be designed with a parking brake that engages automatically when the engine stops, or that the operator may engage manually, to prevent undesirable weight cart motion. The parking brake must be capable of restraining the cart at the maximum gross weight under normal operating conditions.

The parking brake and service brake may be the same system, provided both functions are performed.

4.20   Directional Controls

All operator controls shall be permanently and unambiguously labeled as to the expected weight cart response with an indicated operator input.

4.21   Battery *

Batteries used to provide power to the motor for starting or propulsion shall be of the sealed lead acid type. The battery shall be placed for ease of maintenance and have a means of installing a wire seal to indicate tampering, adjustment or replacement. The wire seal must be placed to allow safety inspections and routine maintenance such as terminal cleaning. The weight cart must be submitted for recalibration if the battery is replaced.

4.22   Battery Charging Circuit

The battery charging circuit shall regulate the charging voltage and current at a level suitable for the battery in use to avoid mass instabilities caused by venting through the battery case pressure relief mechanism.

4.23   Routine Lubrication

All lubrication points must be accessible from a safe location around the cart while it is parked on a flat surface. Routine maintenance shall not require that the weight cart be suspended from a hoist to perform routine lubrication. The design shall allow easy removal of excess or displaced lubricant after servicing.

4.24   Electrical Power Connections

External electrical power required by weight carts with electric motors shall be supplied via a detachable power cord from either a truck mounted generation system or from facility power. The power connections shall be made using electrical connectors that are Underwriters Laboratories approved and that conform to local electrical codes. It is recommended that electrical code requirements be investigated prior to manufacture of the cart.

Only those electrical connectors permanently mounted to the weight cart structure shall be included in the calibrated mass of the weight cart. All removable electrical connectors shall be removed during calibration and at any time when the calibrated mass of the weight cart is referenced or used.

Any upgrades or changes required by changes in the local electrical code requires that the weight cart be submitted for recalibration prior to use.

4.25   Remote Operation

Remote operation of the weight cart may require the addition of actuators and radio frequency receiving units. The installation of such components shall not interfere with compliance with this handbook.

5 Tolerances *

The tolerances in Table 1 are the maximum allowed if the standard is to be used without correction in scale testing applications. Weight carts should be adjusted during calibration to nominal values when possible.

Table 1. Tolerances

Nominal Empty Weight (lb)	Weight Cart Tolerance (± lb)
2000	0.50
2500	0.50
3000	1.00
3500	1.00
4000	1.25
4500	1.25
5000	1.50
5500	1.50
6000	2.00

The assigned weight cart tolerances are based on an evaluation of the expanded uncertainty of the scale calibration as compared with one third of the current scale maintenance and acceptance tolerances (from NIST Handbook 44 tolerance tables applied to the device being tested). The sum of the maximum allowable error of the weight cart plus the allowable errors of the weights required to perform the test shall be used to evaluate test loads for compliance to Handbook 44 requirements.

6 Verification Requirements
6.1 Legal Requirements

The specifications and tolerances specified in this handbook are intended to permit the use of weight carts in normal field-testing operations as field standards having nominal values. Weights and measures requirements, including but not limited to, inspection, testing, and sealing, by a NIST WMD Recognized laboratory shall be followed.

NOTE: Some States have requirements that are not documented here. Check with your local jurisdiction for requirements.

6.2 Initial Verification

A weight cart shall be inspected and calibrated before being placed in service to ensure that the specifications and tolerances of this handbook are met. The calibration status of a weight cart shall be verified as often as required by regulation or circumstance, especially when damage is known or suspected.

6.3   Periodic Calibration

Field standards must be verified prior to use and rechecked as often as regulations or circumstances require, especially when damage is known or suspected or seals are broken. Initial weight cart calibration intervals shall be established at 1 year and extended or reduced based on historical evidence, up to the limit determined by State or local regulations. The calibration interval should not exceed 2 years due to the many variable mass components.

6.4   Traceability

Field standards used for legal metrology must be traceable to national standards by calibration in a laboratory recognized under the NIST WMD Laboratory Recognition Program to calibrate in that parameter, range, and scope or a calibration laboratory authorized by a W&M jurisdiction to calibrate field standards.

All components of the weight cart that are not an integral part of the structure shall be sealed to the weight cart structure by means of a wire seal or by use of a tamper indicating material such as an inspection seal lacquer. These include but are not limited to: the battery, motor, hydraulic pump, fluid fill caps, drive motors and oil filter. Removal or replacement of any of these items shall be recorded in the maintenance log of the weight cart.

6.5   Calibration Reports

Acceptable accuracy and traceability to national or international standards shall be documented in a calibration report meeting the requirements of NIST Handbook 143, State Weights and Measures Laboratories Program Handbook.

An 'Inspection Checklist' must accompany the Calibration Report for all weight carts. (See sample checklist in NIST Handbook 145, SOP 33, "Recommended SOP for Calibration of Weight Carts").

7   Test Methods
7.1   Documented Test Procedure

Calibration of weight carts shall be by an approved NIST procedure, NIST Handbook 145, SOP 33, "Recommended SOP for Calibration of Weight Carts." Additional requirements may be established by the jurisdiction in which the weight cart will be used.

8   Uncertainties

Uncertainties of the calibration must be evaluated according to the ISO Guide to the Expression of Uncertainty in Measurement, 1993. The expanded uncertainty (k=2) of the calibration must be less than one-third of the tolerance specified for the weight cart being tested and be evaluated to ensure that the three to one accuracy ratio required by NIST Handbook 44 is maintained.

Typical uncertainty components for calibration that should be considered are: scale/balance standard deviation, uncertainty of standards and such other measurement influences that are determined to be significant to the weight cart calibration process.

9 User Requirements

9.1 Use In Combination With Test Weights

A weight cart may be used, alone or in combination with Class F field standard weights, up to the maximum gross weight established by the manufacturer. The user must ensure that the requirements of NIST HB 44 are maintained. Compliance with NIST HB 105-8 does not guarantee suitability of a weight cart to test a specific weighing device at all test loads. Each test load must be evaluated for compliance with the requirements of NIST Handbook 44, Appendix A, "Fundamental Considerations," Section 3, "Testing Apparatus." The combined tolerance of the weight cart plus the tolerance of any weights used on the cart must be less than one-third of the scale tolerance to be applied $\left(T_{cart} + T_{weights} < \dfrac{T_{scale}}{3} \right)$. This determination of suitability is especially critical for testing Class III scales, having division sizes 'd' = 5 lb or 'd' = 10 lb, to acceptance tolerances.

9.2 Weight Cart Maintenance

Any maintenance process performed between scheduled calibrations altering the mass of the weight cart invalidates the calibrated mass of the cart and requires that the weight cart be recalibrated. This includes, but is not limited to: replacement of the battery, changing lubricating oil and filter, and servicing of the hydraulic system. When "As Found" data is required for reverse traceability, maintenance should be performed after measuring and recording the "As Found" mass of the weight cart. For this test, only the fuel level shall be adjusted. All other fluid levels shall remain as they were when the cart was delivered for calibration. "Final" calibration data shall be recorded after completion of routine maintenance, adjustment of all fluid levels, and any other adjustments.

9.3 Weight Cart Maintenance Log

The organization owning the weight cart shall establish a maintenance log containing a detailed record of all maintenance performed on the weight cart. The log should document serial numbers of individually serialized weight cart components, e.g. engine, hydraulic pump, battery and drive motors. The log will include copies of all Calibration Reports and completed Inspection Checklists, as well as fuel tank conformance certificates, if appropriate. This log shall document the calibration status and history of the weight cart beginning at the time of initial placement in service to the current time of use. The Maintenance Log of weight carts placed in service prior to publication of Handbook 105-8 shall begin as of the date of Handbook 105-8 publication and shall include such previous documentation as is available. Documentation of maintenance shall include a description of the maintenance performed, including part numbers and serial numbers where applicable, and when available, the weight of items removed from or installed on the weight cart.

9.4 Inspection Checklist Verification

Prior to a scale test, all items on the Inspection Checklist must be evaluated for consistency with conditions at calibration. All fluids must be at the levels recorded at the time of calibration and all tires must be in good condition.

9.5   Weight Cart Cleanliness

The weight cart shall be maintained free of all visible contamination; this includes but is not limited to: mud, lubricants, water or product being weighed.

9.6   User Modifications

User modifications of weight carts are discouraged. However, it is recognized that modifications, e.g., installation of warning beacons, may be required.   Such modifications performed by or at the request of weight cart users must be permanent changes to the weight cart, and become a fixed part of the weight cart structure. Items that are part of such modifications and which may be easily removed must be permanently attached to the weight cart using wire seals or tamper indicating materials, as required in section 6.4. Modifications must be documented in the maintenance log as required in section 9.3 and include a list of materials and drawings that detail the modification. The weight cart shall be recalibrated and adjusted to the nominal empty weight specified on the manufacturer's identification plate upon completion of any modifications. If adjustment to the original nominal empty weight is not feasible, the weight cart should be adjusted to the lowest possible nominal empty weight from paragraph 4.1.1 and a new identification plate procured that reflects the new nominal empty weight.

9.7   Licensing of Weight Cart Operators (Informational)

According to the U.S. Department of Labor, Occupational Safety and Health Administration (OSHA) web page, a weight cart *may* be considered to be a Powered Industrial Truck. Owning organizations and operators should contact the office of OSHA responsible for their operational area for a written determination of the weight cart status. More information can be obtained from: OSHA, Directorate of Safety Standards Programs; U.S. DEPARTMENT OF LABOR; Room N3621; 200 Constitution Avenue, N.W; Washington, D.C. 20210. Telephone (202) 693-2082; FAX (202) 693-1663. If the weight cart is designated a Powered Industrial Truck, the operator must complete an operator training course, and a daily safety inspection and checklist are required. A sample checklist is provided as Attachment 2. Use of a similar checklist is suggested for all weight carts, regardless of OSHA status, to assist in maintaining good maintenance records.

Figure 1
Typical Liquid Fuel Powered Weight Cart Configurations

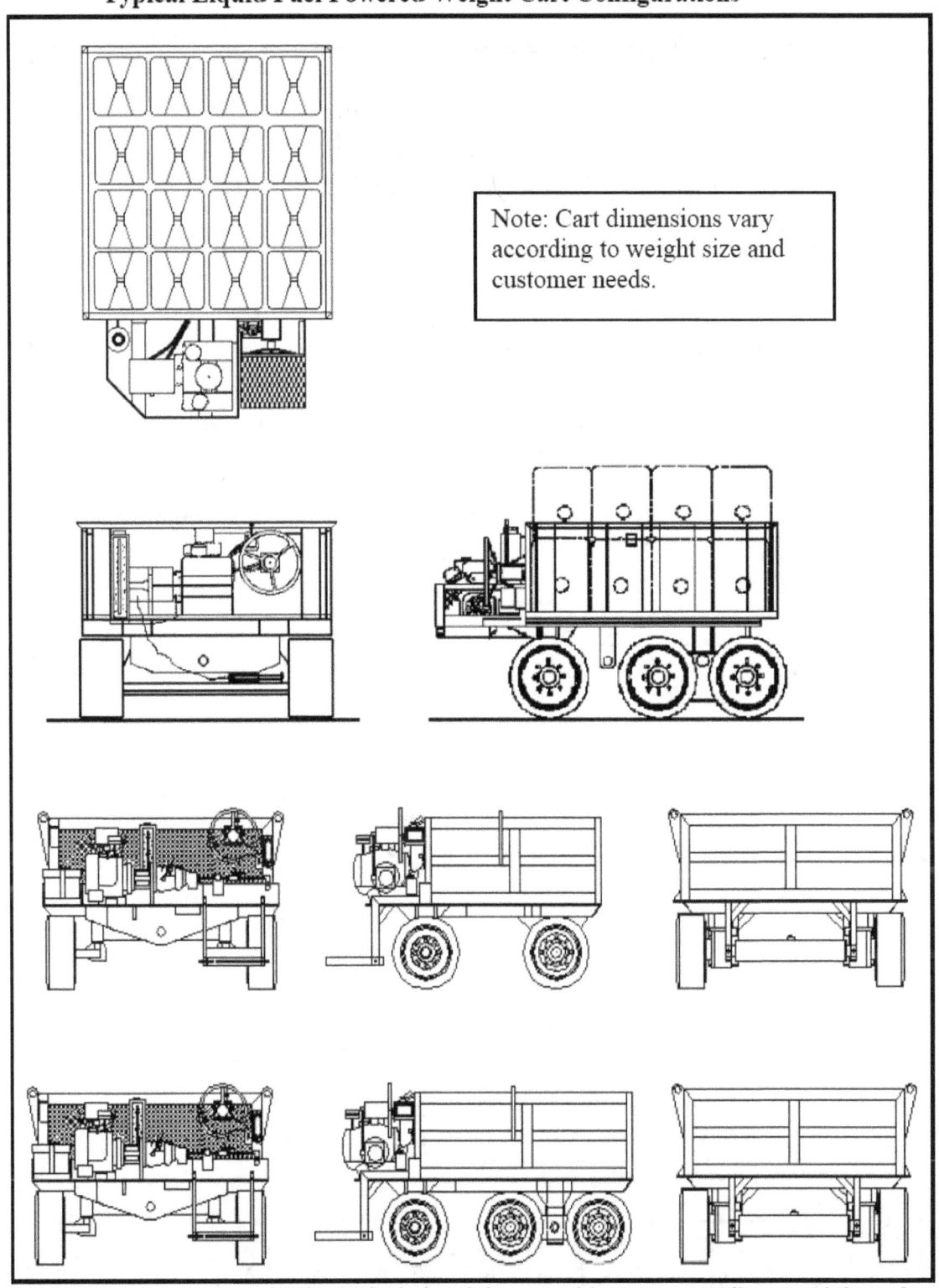

Note: Cart dimensions vary according to weight size and customer needs.

Typical configurations of a liquid fueled weight cart with up to 6 000 lb net weight and up to 37 500 lb gross weight.

Figure 2
Typical Electrically Powered Weight Cart Configurations

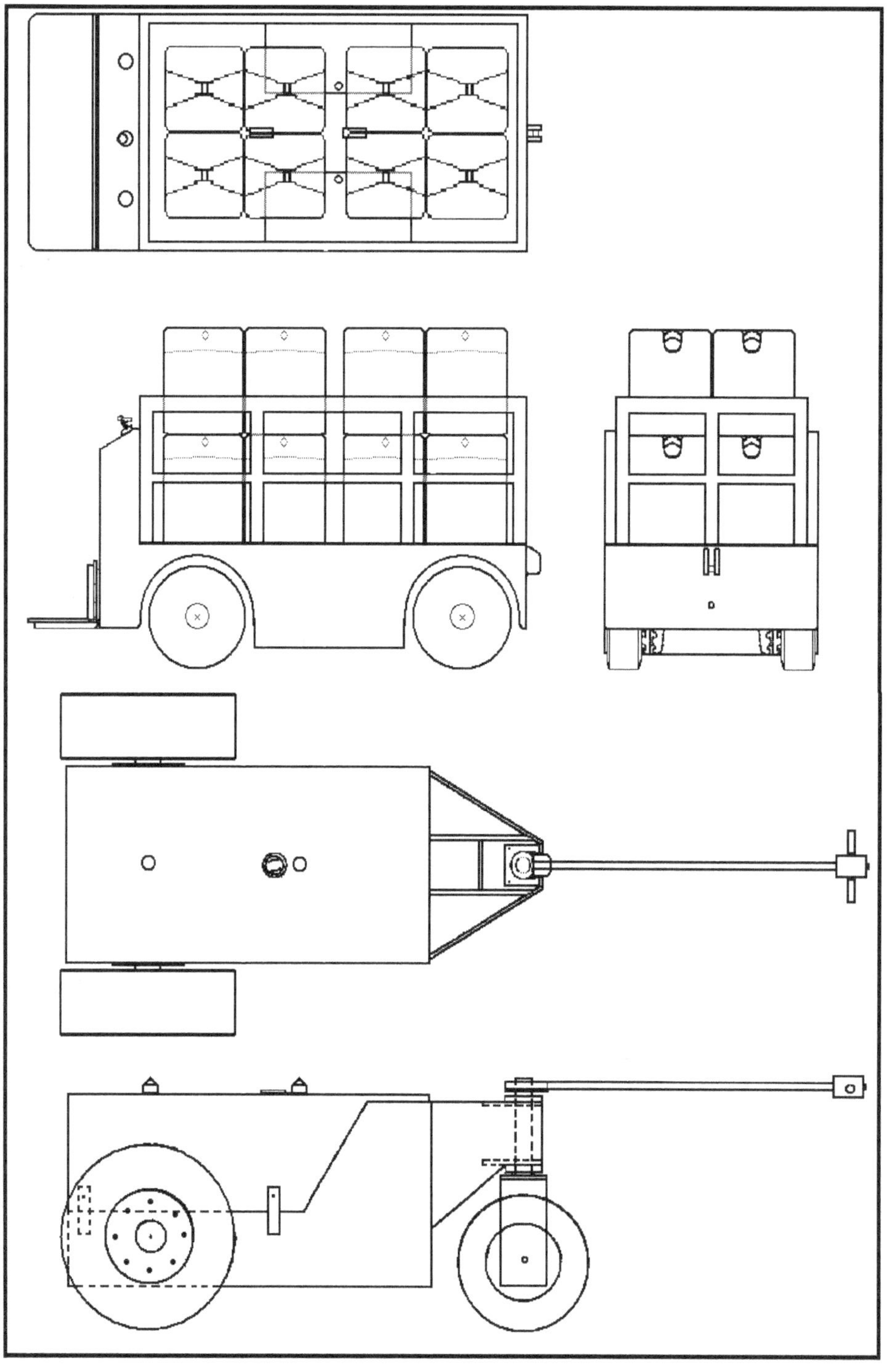

Typical configurations of electrically (battery) powered weight carts with up to 4 000 lb net weight and up to 20 000 lb gross weight.

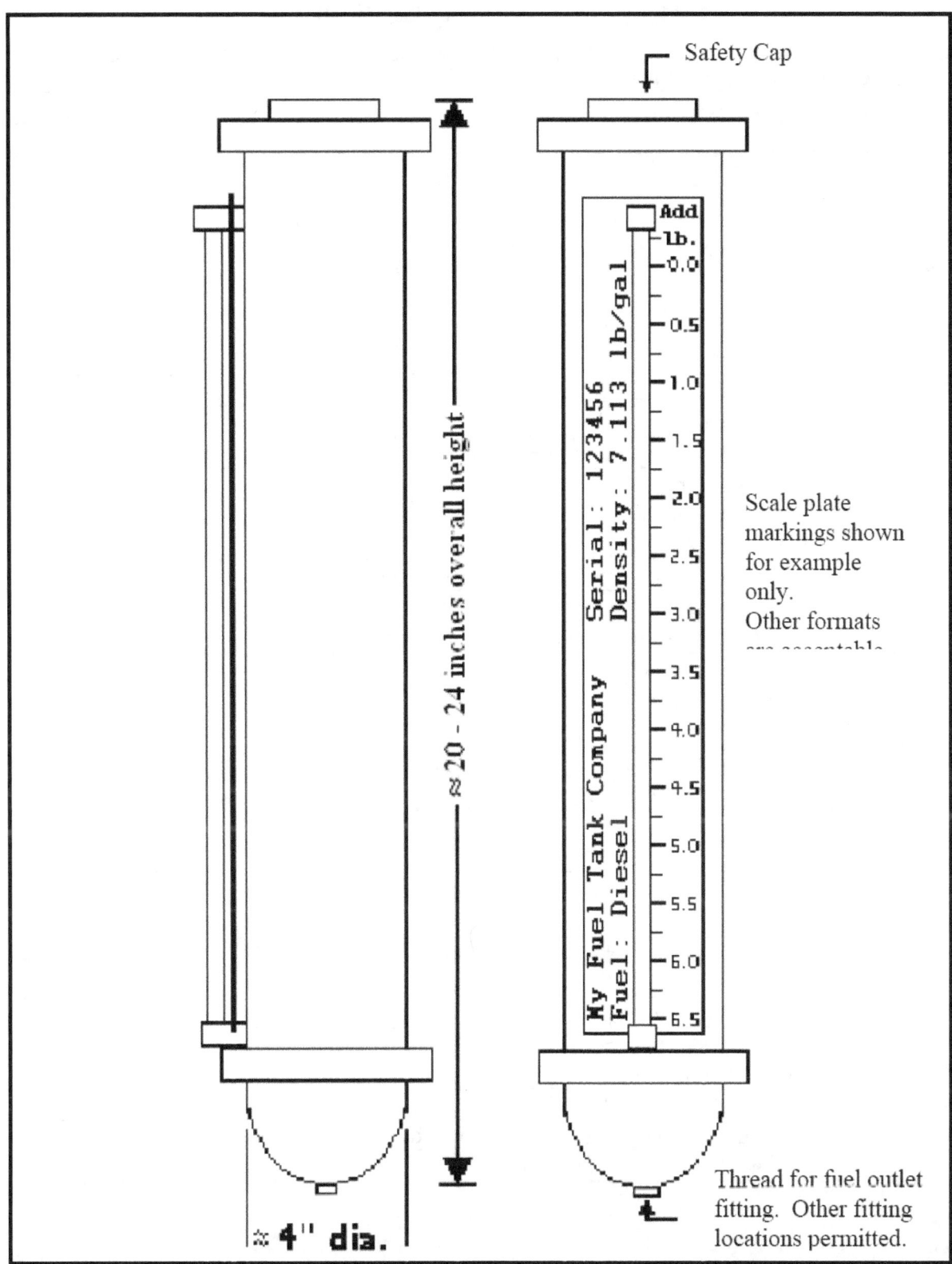

Safety Cap

≈ 20 - 24 inches overall height

Add
lb.
0.0
0.5
1.0
1.5
2.0
2.5
3.0
3.5
4.0
4.5
5.0
5.5
6.0
6.5

My Fuel Tank Company   Serial: 123456
Fuel: Diesel   Density: 7.113 lb/gal

Scale plate
markings shown
for example
only.
Other formats

Thread for fuel outlet
fitting. Other fitting
locations permitted.

≈ 4" dia.

Attachment 2
Example Daily Weight Cart Inspection Checklist
(Must be altered to fit the weight cart in use)

Weight cart identification number	
Weight cart manufacturer	
Weight cart model number	
Weight cart serial number	

Walk Around				
	(OK)	(Inspection starts at operator platform)	Needs Attention	Date Corrected
1.		No evidence of metal fatigue on cart structure (e.g. cracks)		
2.		No evidence of fluid leaks		
3.		Tire Integrity (e.g. major nicks, cracks, cuts contamination)		
4.		Wheels secured		
5.		Major components secured in place (e.g. Engine, battery, fuel tank, hydraulic pump)		
6.		Engine oil level correct and oil not grossly contaminated		
7.		Hydraulic oil level correct and oil not grossly contaminated		
8.		Operator platform level and securely attached		
9.		All guards and shields in place and secure		
10.		Steering components securely attached		
11.		All tamper indicators in place		
12.		Fuel tank filled to proper level		
13.		All labels and decals in place		

Operational Checklist				
	(OK)	(Start weight cart motor and test controls)	Needs Attention	Date Corrected
1.		Engine starts and operates properly		
2.		Steering mechanism works properly		
3.		No fluid leaks		
4.		Forward/reverse controls functioning properly		
5.		Warning beacons functional (if equipped)		
6.		Rail gear functional (if equipped)